SOAR

A COMPANION WORKBOOK TO "HUSH"
FOR PERSONAL AND GROUP STUDY

NICOLE BRADDOCK BROMLEY

SOAR
A COMPANION WORKBOOK TO "HUSH" FOR
PERSONAL AND GROUP STUDY

iUniverse books may be ordered through booksellers or by contacting:

iUniverse
1663 Liberty Drive
Bloomington, IN 47403
www.iuniverse.com
1-800-Authors (1-800-288-4677)

Because of the dynamic nature of the Internet, any web addresses or links contained in this book may have changed since publication and may no longer be valid. The views expressed in this work are solely those of the author and do not necessarily reflect the views of the publisher, and the publisher hereby disclaims any responsibility for them.

ISBN: 978-1-4917-2520-7 (sc)
ISBN: 978-1-4917-2521-4 (e)

Library of Congress Control Number: 2014902540

Print information available on the last page.

iUniverse rev. date: 02/22/2019

CONTENTS

INTRODUCTION

SOAR is a workbook and video companion to my first book, *Hush: Moving from Silence to Healing after Childhood Sexual Abuse* (Moody Publishers, 2007). I wrote it after reading thousands of emails from sexual abuse survivors, many of them telling me that *Hush* has had an incredible impact on their lives and that they wished they could connect with other survivors in a group setting.

I want that for you, too! My heart longs for you to find freedom from your pain by breaking the silence, realizing that what happened to you wasn't your fault and that you're not alone. I also want to help you personally apply the teachings of *Hush* in a practical way, to journal the things you've been afraid to share, to make it easy for you to talk with others walking on the same path, and to connect you with the God of all comfort, who walks with you toward that pinpoint light of hope at the end of a dark tunnel.

Referring to *Hush* frequently as you work through *SOAR* will help you understand the common effects, struggles, and pain associated with sexual abuse. This workbook is meant to be a friend in that process, holding your hand and helping you take a deep look inside yourself to see how abuse has affected your life, worldview, and relationships and how you want those things to look in the future.

SOAR is both a personal and group study. It's designed for sexual abuse survivors who long for healing and want a support community to encourage and guide them on their journey. It's for those who want more than to merely survive. It's for those who want to thrive—to soar above their circumstances. The goal is not to completely heal your pain, as I do not believe that is possible until Jesus takes us home. However, I do believe that this study will help you step out of your closet of silence and onto the healing path He has for you. I also believe that along the way, you will not only find your voice, but will also experience freedom from the shame and purpose beyond the pain.

HOW TO USE THIS WORKBOOK

SOAR is broken up into seven sessions. Each week you'll read one or two chapters of *Hush* and then flip open your *SOAR* journal to follow some writing prompts that will help you apply the chapter topics to your own journey. You'll also learn more about God and begin to connect with Him in your healing.

SOAR follows the four major steps of moving from silence to healing after childhood sexual abuse, as outlined in *Hush*. Sessions 1 and 2 focus on the first step: shattering the silence. Sessions 3 and 4 focus on overcoming the lies that enter our lives as a result of abuse. Session 5 is all about accepting freedom through forgiveness. Sessions 6 and 7 round out the process by dealing with the fourth step of healing: reaching out.

"Soul Work," the personal side of the study, is to help you put on paper some of the things you've bottled up inside. Journaling is crucial for healing and health. You can write in the spaces provided or buy your own blank journal. The point is to have as much as space as you need to write, draw, scribble and express yourself and your story on paper as much as you can.

Once you've done your weekly Soul Work, you'll be ready to meet with your support group. "Circle Work" is relationship-based and conversation-focused, so come ready to leave your masks at the door. In a safe, nonjudgmental, understanding, grace—and mercy-filled space, we encourage open, honest sharing about the real issues you're struggling with. Here's a place where you get to be yourself! And if you don't know who that is yet, now is the time to find out. You are to come as you are and will be accepted as you are. Just be willing to commit to the Soul Work each week, attend the group meetings, and share as you are able to. God will meet you in this.

The support, validation, understanding, strength, and compassion that can be found in such a group setting is something you won't find anywhere else. It may take time for you to feel ready to share, and that's okay. Healing is a lifelong journey, and baby steps mean a lot. There's no pressure to meet certain expectations by the end of the study. Some of you will grow to incredible heights as each session progresses; others might feel able to take only a couple of steps forward even after seven sessions. Either way, you will see positive change and forward movement, and your progress will empower you to continue your journey, perhaps by joining another *SOAR* group and working through the process again. The more you're able to open up in your circle, the stronger your wings will become.

There are seven short videos that correspond to the study sessions. I serve as your video host and some of my survivor friends share their stories, too. In a group setting, these short films will help break the ice and introduce the week's topic, but even if you aren't in a group yet these videos can still be used to bring a level of comfort and understanding as you work through the personal side of the study. These short films can be purchased and downloaded from the online store at iamonevoice.org.

I'm proud of you for making the decision to work through this workbook. It's an honor to journey with you at a deeper level. May God prepare our minds, ready our hearts, give us courage, strengthen our wings, and bless our steps ahead.

Now, let's begin to

SOAR!

SESSION 1

SHATTERING
THE SILENCE

READ: *HUSH*, CHAPTER ONE

Hello!

I'm so excited that you've decided to work through this study with me! I'm also incredibly proud of you for taking the huge step of joining a group of people who truly care about those who have been affected by sexual abuse and may likely have survived it themselves.

You probably opened this book with questions about who you are, what your purpose is, why you do the things you do and feel the way you feel. Remember that while what happened to you in the past affects you, it doesn't define you. Your story is still being written. And, since this is your personal journey of healing and you get to make your own choices along the way, there are a few things you can do to make the process more beneficial.

First, like anything worth doing well, *SOAR* requires time, energy, and commitment. Be willing to set limits in your everyday life in order to care for yourself as you give this process priority. It's also important that you go at your own pace. You can work through this book quickly, or you can take it slow. If you haven't committed to a group yet, you can stop journaling after a few sessions, put the workbook down for a season, or take small breaks anytime you want.

Second, this study invites a willingness to struggle, question, and feel. Allow yourself the freedom to cry, yell, draw, write, pray, skip questions, highlight words, cross out sections, crumple up pages, throw the book, hug it, cuddle, or trash it all together.

Above all else, make sure you keep yourself safe as you work through this book and meet with your group. Perhaps you've already found healthy ways of creating safety and safe routines in your life, but it's likely that in every group there will be some who have not. And there will certainly be survivors who have never told a soul about their little secret because they never had a safe person to tell it to. Others may have tried to tell their secret, only to find that the person they trusted didn't believe them or told them to "hush," leading them to believe the lie that people can't be trusted and that no one is safe enough to handle their secret.

In *SOAR*, we challenge these lies and learn to reach out to others to create safe support systems. Before we begin, take a moment to list some people, places, and things that help you feel safe, calm, or grounded when you're feeling upset or overwhelmed. Examples might be calling a specific person who makes you feel safe, a certain type of music, scripture, meditation, medication, a blanket, warm bath, exercise, or painting.

As you create safety for yourself on this difficult road, I hope you can let yourself really engage in every step ahead. Allow the Lord and His people to speak life into your journey. Change, strength, truth, and freedom are on the horizon. It's time to gather new tools that will enable you to stand up, step out, gain momentum and, in time, SOAR down the path ahead!

May the silence be broken and may God bless your journey,
Nicole

SOUL WORK

Digging Deep

Now that you've read the introduction and first chapter of *Hush*, think about whether or not any of the stories resonated with you.

Can you relate to Shelby? Do you know anyone like her? Describe any similarities you find between yourself and Shelby or between her and someone you know.

Can you relate to my story in any way at this point? Why or why not?

Think about what life was like for you as you were growing up. Answer as many of the following questions as you can.

What was your family like?

With whom did you live?

With whom did you feel safe?

Whom could you trust?

With whom did you spend the most time?

Where did you play the most?

What did you play?

Where did you find yourself feeling happiest? Most loved? Most accepted?

What made you feel valued?

Were you ever told as a child that you had to keep something a secret?

As a mother of young children, I try to be very intentional, yet sensitive, about the way I teach my kids about the body, safe relationships, and abuse. As part of that, I want them to understand the difference between secrets and surprises.

What words or pictures come to your mind when you think of surprises?

What words or pictures come to mind when you think of secrets?

Personally, I think of a surprise as something playful and joyful that generates excitement in anticipation of something wonderful that will be revealed in the future. It's something that can be shared with others at the right time. A secret, on the other hand, excludes others, usually because telling it would engender anger, hurt feelings, or sadness. Secrets can never be told.

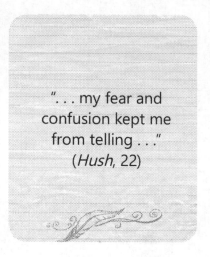

"... my fear and confusion kept me from telling ..." (*Hush*, 22)

Sexual perpetrators often tell their victims that what they are doing is a secret that they can never tell. My stepfather always called it "our little secret," and it certainly felt that way. I wanted to tell, but at the same time I was too afraid.

Is there a secret you've been afraid to tell?

- ☐ For sure
- ☐ Yeah, probably
- ☐ Not that I can recall

Being willing to admit that there's a secret that could be holding you hostage is the first step on the road to freedom.

In *Hush*, I talk about feeling as if there was no way out and making myself believe that the abuse was normal, telling myself that I had to endure the molestation in order to keep my family together. Can you relate to any of that? Was there something you forced your mind to believe in order to survive by keeping the secret?

Wisdom from the Word

Read Psalm 39:2.

The writer of this verse wanted to keep silent. He was unsure about what God was doing. He didn't understand what was going on, and he couldn't seem to trust those around him. As a result, he told himself that keeping silent was the best thing to do. Do you ever feel like that?

You have just set out on an incredible, life-changing journey, and I know that as you take that first step, you may be feeling really shaky. But your journey begins by understanding the power of the secret you've locked away inside yourself. Maybe you tried to tell it at some point, only to be rejected, told to hush, or ignored, so you locked it back up. As much as you try to convince yourself that it's best to keep silent, you also know that your secret is tearing you up inside.

Crying Out to God

God wants to enter our story, listen to our laments, and comfort our hearts. David, the author of most of the Psalms, knew this, and time after time he poured out his feelings to the Lord. Check out any of these Psalms: 3, 4, 5, 7, 9-10, 13, 14, 17, 22, 25, 26, 27, 28, 31, 36, 39, 40:12-17, 41, 42-43, 52, 53, 54, 55, 56, 57, 59, 61, 64, 69, 70, 71, 77, 86, 89, 120, 139, 141, 142. These "Psalms of Lament" show us what a straightforward conversation with God might sound like.

It's important to note that the writer isn't concerned about how he *should* or *should not* be feeling. Instead, he honestly pours out the feelings that are inside of him. The truth is that these feelings are going to come out somehow, whether in relationships or through some form of behavior. Instead of letting shame or negative feelings control us, we can write a lament as a healthy way to release destructive feelings like anger and frustration. We can bring them to God to be dealt with.

Your lament may include things like the following:

☐ Your concern about your own thoughts; for example, the lies you believe or the confusion you struggle with.

☐ The abuse you endured and how it has affected you.

☐ How you really feel about your abuser or someone who you feel didn't protect you. Be honest. Remember, you're trying to bring yourself to God as you are, not as you think you should be.

☐ How all of this has affected the way you view God. If you feel He is distant, tell Him. If you are unsure, tell Him that.

Close your eyes for a moment, take a deep breath, and then begin to write your lament to the Lord. This may take more than one attempt, but it's is one way you can begin to tell your story and get your voice back.

Making It Personal

If you've been sexually violated in any way, I want you to know that you aren't alone. I know this might be really hard for you, but try to answer some of the following questions about your experience. No one else has to see what you write, and you don't have to share anything you write unless you choose to. By starting to think about your secret, you'll begin to understand it, and that understanding will lead you into the pathway of healing you long for.

What do you remember most about your abuse?

When did it begin?

How did it begin?

How did you come to know your
abuser?

What made you keep your abuser's secret?

If the abuse has stopped, when did it stop?

Do you have any idea why it stopped?

If the abuse hasn't stopped, I want to encourage you to speak to your group leader, a counselor, or someone else you trust. No one deserves abuse—it is not your fault. There are people who want to help you be safe and get help.

As you work through this study, you might be worried about the ramifications of telling parts of your secret, even on paper. Remember that in this study and in the group you meet with, we are all committed to confidentiality. You don't have to share, but the more you're able to, the more others will, and the more healing and freedom you will all be able to experience. Unlocked secrets lead to freedom from shame, which in turn leads to wholeness and becoming everything you were meant to be.

CIRCLE WORK

Getting Real

Share with the group at least one answer from the questions at the beginning of this week's Soul Work about how you grew up. This will help others get to know a little more about you and your background.

Story Time

In chapter 1 of *Hush*, I mention that someone came to my school and showed an awareness video about childhood sexual abuse. Have you ever seen something like that at your school or church? Talk about the first time you heard about sexual abuse. How did you become aware of it? Was it a good experience or a bad one? Can you remember your thoughts about it at that time? Share what you felt, thought, or did in response.

In the sessions to come, a part of Circle Work will be set aside for the participants to share their stories. This is one of the most important times for you in this study, and I hope you'll begin thinking now about what it might take for you to get real with those in your safe circle.

Creative Moment

Draw something that represents your secret, if you have acknowledged having one, and how it makes you feel. If you think you haven't had a secret, draw a picture of what it might feel like to have one.

Be creative and free with the art supplies provided. No one has to know what your picture is really about if you aren't ready to talk about it.

Prayer Ministry

The group leader will ask group participants to pray silently in response to each of the prompts below as she reads them aloud.

- Ask the Lord to begin a new work in you.
- Ask Him to make you ready to say "yes" to Him, even if it's hard work.
- Tell Him what you are tired of. Ask Him for strength.
- Tell Him you want Him to restore your voice. Ask Him to make you a voice for others.

Some of you may be very angry at God and have absolutely no desire to pray. That's okay. God understands. He is also angry at what happened to you. Out of respect for others who want to pray, please just look at your lap while they do.

Close the session with this prayer.

Father God,

As we take this first step on our healing journey,

we invite You to be with us.

We cast our feelings and anxieties upon You,

knowing that You want to heal us.

Thank You for sending Your Son to destroy secret and shameful ways

and to bring truth and light to replace the lies and darkness and secrets

that have kept us from fulfilling our dreams

and Your plan for us.

In Jesus's name,

Amen

SESSION 2

SHATTERING
THE SILENCE
(CONTINUED)

READ: *HUSH*, CHAPTERS TWO AND THREE

SOUL WORK

Digging Deep

In the first session, you began thinking about your story: what you remember about your abuse, when it began, how it began, when it stopped, and where you are now. In this session, the focus is on identifying the lies that have entered your life as a result of abuse, especially the lies that have kept you silent.

Your goal is to move from hiding behind those lies, allowing them to affect your relationships and thought patterns, to exposing them to the light and replacing them with the truth. Shattering the silence of the lies you have believed brings freedom and wholeness.

Review the lies on pages 30-33 of *Hush*.

Which ones jump out at you?

> "Identifying the lies that fuel our fears can help us find the courage to tell."
> (*Hush*, 34)

Have you personally struggled with these or other lies that aren't listed, like "it was my fault, because . . .

Use the space below to write out the lies you can identify in connection with your abuse.

The lie about the situation:

The lie about me:

The lie about my life:

The lie about others:

The lie about God:

What do you think the truth is? Don't feel you need to address everything on the list; just concentrate on those that seem to fit your experience. If you aren't sure about the truth right now, that's okay. You'll have an opportunity to process it during the group portion of the study.

The truth about the situation:

The truth about me:

The truth about my life:

The truth about others:

The truth about God:

Now that you've spent some time identifying and refuting some of the lies that have bound you, let's address the biggest lie of all: that you must *hush*. Read Acts 18:1-11.

What was Paul up against?

What did God tell Paul to do?

What did Paul do?

What was the result?

I remember the first time I read Acts 18:9 and how this truth tugged at my heart. I believe that God is telling us the same thing He told Paul. *We don't have to be afraid to speak out!*

Realizing that you don't have to be afraid is one of the most important steps in your healing journey. Those who oppose God and His truth will say and do everything they can to keep you silent and bound in the chains of secrets and lies. But God is calling you to embrace truth and to speak out. He wants you to find your voice! He wants you to shatter the silence because He wants you to be free!

Breaking the silence is the first step of healing from childhood sexual abuse. It takes a lot of courage, and it may be the hardest thing you've ever done in your life, but it's worth it. You are worth it.

Take some time to journal about telling your secret. Maybe you have broken your silence and the response of the one you believed you could trust wasn't what you hoped for or deserved. Write about that experience and what it might take for you to find the courage to tell again. Maybe you've never told and this is your first opportunity to take the biggest, most courageous step on your healing journey. Write about what that feels like and what you hope to gain from it.

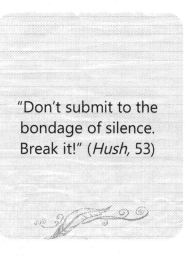

"Don't submit to the bondage of silence. Break it!" (*Hush*, 53)

Wisdom from the Word

Read Isaiah 28:14-16

What does God say the rulers of His people have done?

What does He say will happen because of this?

What alternative does He offer His people?

God promises to sweep away all lies and to provide a refuge for those who trust in His Son, Jesus Christ. When we have a relationship with Jesus, we don't need to hide behind the secrets and lies that keep us imprisoned in shame. In Him, we find our freedom! Jesus is the key to unlocking the door.

Another word for *falsehood* in verse 15 is "false gods." In and of themselves, these aren't always bad things. They can be friends, food, success, or something else that *in its proper place* can be a healthy thing. But whenever we make anything besides God our refuge, it takes His place in our life and becomes a false god (we will discuss this further in Session 3).

Take some time to quiet yourself and then ask God these questions:

What lie do I cling to instead of clinging to You?

What have I believed as a result of my abuse that is keeping me locked up?

Are there people or things that I use as my hiding place instead of taking refuge under the shadow of Your wings (Ruth 2:12)?

If we continue reading to the end of Isaiah 28, we find the last verse (Isaiah 28:29) telling us that we can take refuge in the Lord because His counsel is wonderful and His wisdom is great. In Him, we find all that we need to rediscover our voice, to shatter the silence surrounding the secrets of our past, and to experience the comfort and freedom we have longed for since the day our abuse began.

"Telling released me from my past so I could embrace the future."
(*Hush,* 52)

Opening Up

Use the empty space below to begin writing your story. You can share as little or as much as you feel comfortable doing. Ask the Lord to show you what to share right now and how to share it. Feel free to be creative.

My story . . . .

If you haven't shared your story with your group yet, begin thinking about what it will take for you to do so. Practice by reading a piece of what you have just written with someone you trust, even if they've heard it before.

CIRCLE WORK

Getting Real

Now that you've watched this week's video opener, share with the group the answers to any of these questions that stood out to you.

- Whose story in the video (or in chapter 2 or 3 of *Hush*) did I relate to the most and why?
- What did I like (or dislike) about this session's homework?
- What has been my biggest fear about breaking the silence?
- What has kept me from telling in the past?

In *Hush,* I wrote: "My shame was overwhelming, and to be free to heal, I needed to go back to when sexual abuse first planted this lie in my soul and allow others to help me replace it with truth" (39). Share one of the biggest lies that you've believed as a result of the abuse you survived. Rewrite the lie here and then write down the responses of your circle members.

Lie:

Responses:

Story Time

After a survivor shares her story, share your reaction with the group. If you feel courage rising up in you to share your own story, talk to your leader about signing up to tell it at the next session.

Creative Moment

Use the crayons, paint, markers, pencils, and paper provided to express either a part of your story or the emotion(s) you feel when you think about breaking the silence. Share your art with the group.

Prayer Ministry

Share prayer requests. Write them down on the next page and remember to pray for them throughout the next week.

As you finish up Circle Work this week, here's a prayer that you may want to pray as a group. If you feel comfortable praying aloud, you might want to offer your own prayer for yourself and the members of your group.

God, thank You that Your Word says that You are with us,
that You are a safe refuge for us,
and that, with You, we do not need to fear.
Thank You that you do not want us to be silent.
Please give us the courage to shatter the silence
surrounding our past.
Lord, please be our strength in keeping our thoughts pure
and obedient to Jesus Christ,
keeping our minds set on truth instead of lies.
Thank you for this community of support.
Help us to share honestly
and to receive the comfort others can give us.
Bless each one of us and protect us on our
personal healing journeys.
By the Holy Spirit, give us the power we need
to speak truth to lies.
In Jesus's name we pray,
Amen.

SESSION 3

OVERCOMING LIES

READ: *HUSH*, CHAPTER FOUR

SOUL WORK

Digging Deep

In our last session, we focused on exposing the lies that keep us silent and prevent us from moving forward on our healing journey. In this session, we'll focus on renouncing the lie that we can't trust God. Believing this lie is common among survivors of abuse, mainly because someone close to you or in authority over you, someone you trusted or should have been able to trust, betrayed you, took advantage you, used and abused you. It's no surprise that you may struggle to ever trust again.

The problem is that when you feel you can't trust anyone, it's easy to believe that you have to rely on your own resources to control your circumstances and cope with your pain. As natural as this may seem, acting on this lie will not only delay your healing, but may also cause you to hurt yourself and others in the process.

> "Your fears can lead you to cope in unhealthy ways that will just perpetuate the bondage that you feel."
> (*Hush*, 53)

Now that you've read chapter 4, take a moment to journal your thoughts and feelings about using your power to disguise, damage, or destroy as a coping mechanism.

Did you relate to the "Control Freak," the "Perfectionist," the "Tough Girl," or the "People Pleaser"?

How have you tried to disguise your pain?

Have you ever purposely harmed yourself in some way?

Have you seen a pattern in the ways you've hurt others in your life?

Have you ever thought of ending your life?

Which of these coping mechanisms have you relied on the most?

Consider Hope's letter for a moment. Which part resonated with you as you read her story? Do you think God could do such beautiful things in your own life? If not, do you think it's because you don't believe you can trust Him? Get real with yourself and journal your thoughts.

Wisdom from the Word

Read Zechariah 4.

In this chapter, God is trying to encourage His people through prophetic visions and a conversation between Zechariah and an angel. After a long period of captivity in Babylon, a band of Jews under the leadership of Zerubbabel had returned to the Promised Land to rebuild the temple. But when they saw the extent of the destruction, their hearts sank. It seemed an impossible task for any human to carry out. What does the Lord say in verse 6?

What does it mean to you to do something by your own might and power?

Looking back at the thoughts you recorded about your ability to disguise, damage, or destroy, do you think you were trying to cope with your circumstances by relying on your own power and might? What was the result?

How does God say a seemingly impossible task can be accomplished?

Trusting in God's power rather than your own can be difficult for those who have experienced abuse. His power isn't what we expect because it isn't rooted in selfishness or a desire to control, but rather in His commitment to us and our restoration. Over and over, God's Word tells us that He loves us, that He is all-powerful, and that He is completely trustworthy. As you begin to understand that God wants to help you heal, you'll also start to see that He can be trusted. It's okay if you don't feel it yet; that will come. Feelings follow beliefs; they cannot lead us. If feelings are leading us, we'll be on the wrong path before we know it!

Friend, if you've grown used to relying on your own power, God is inviting you to come to Him. If you find yourself believing that your healing is all up to you, I encourage you to write out Zechariah 4:6. Post it in your car, on your mirror, in your locker, on your phone's lock screen—anywhere you can see it and be reminded that it's not in your own power to accomplish any of it.

It might make human sense to use your own power to try to disguise your pain, keep silent, or even to try to heal, but now you know that such attempts don't work because they are based on the lie that God can't be trusted. Right now, God is inviting you to trust in Him. He wants to lead you down the best path for your life. You aren't going to accomplish your healing through your own might or power, but solely through God's Spirit.

Do you think you're ready to take God at His word? Maybe this is your moment! Choose to believe that Jesus came to earth and died so that the abuse, the sin against you, and even the sinful ways you've responded to your abuse don't have the final say. Tell Him you want to commit your life to Him as He has committed His life to you, and admit that you need His help to trust Him. Consider writing this down in your own words or drawing a picture of what that looks or feels like to you.

Opening Up

Just as survivors of abuse often find it difficult to trust God, they can also have trouble trusting others. Yet to fully embrace healing and freedom, you need to begin to try to trust others with the real you.

This is what your circle is all about—community and transparency. Before you meet with your group this week, choose someone in your life that you feel you can trust (ask God to help you with this), and reach out to him or her. Tell this person how you are doing and what you learned from this session of the study. Jot down a few possible talking points.

> "My shame was overwhelming, and to be free to heal, I needed to go back to when sexual abuse first planted this lie in my soul and to allow others to help me replace it with the truth."
> *(Hush,* 39)

Find a small object to act as a symbol of one of your most painful memories. It could be something that would seem insignificant to anyone else but has deep significance for you. For example, if you were abused during a vacation at the beach, you might choose a seashell or a sand dollar. Show it to the person you have chosen to trust and share a bit about the memory associated with it and/or how you are asking God to heal that memory. Take it with you when you meet in your circle.

CIRCLE WORK

Getting Real

Watch this week's video opener and discuss as a group:

- ☐ Whose story in chapter 4 of *Hush* or this session's video did I relate to most and why?

- ☐ What did I like (or dislike) about this session's Soul Work?

- ☐ What is it that I know I cannot heal or overcome unless God's power and might is at work in my life?

- ☐ What do I most want God to heal in my life?

Write down your answers even if you aren't ready to reveal them to others. If you feel comfortable sharing them, keep in mind that doing so might just give others the courage to share as well. Allow your circle to provide feedback and encouragement and record their responses here.

Story Time

Listen lovingly to a fellow survivor as she shares her story today. If you feel you're nearly ready to break your own silence, talk to your leader about telling your story in the next meeting.

Creative Moment

Pull out the symbolic object you chose earlier this week and take a moment to share its meaning with the group. Were you able to meet with a friend this week to talk? If so, with whom did you talk? How did it go?

As an act of trust, hand your symbolic object to the person to your left for her to hold for the remainder of the session. If you were holding someone else's symbol, return it to that person at the end of the group time, and as you do, consider asking her how you can pray specifically for this individual this week. This is a picture of what it means to be in a community of survivors, taking steps toward trusting others with our real self and the painful parts of our story.

Prayer Ministry

Take a moment to close your eyes and picture yourself in the Garden of Gethsemane, alone with Jesus. While everyone's eyes are closed, have one person read Matthew 26:36-42 aloud and then ask the following questions:

- ☐ Can you hear Jesus's struggle to trust the Father?
- ☐ Do you hear Him admit his pain, loneliness, and weakness?

☐ Can you hear Him choose to trust the Father anyway?

As you picture yourself in this scene, take a few moments to honestly tell the Father about your own struggle. Don't hold back. He can handle it. Write it out in the space below, draw it, or just say it in your heart. He is listening.

Close in this sample prayer or in a circle member's prayer.

God, sometimes it is so hard
to allow You to be in control of my life.
Sometimes I feel unsafe and struggle to trust You,
so I try to control things myself.
I am ready for things to be different,
but I need Your help, Your power, and
Your strength in order to grow and change and heal.
I choose to trust You today, Lord
(even if it's hard and I don't feel like it),
and I invite You to increase my faith in You.
Please be my Lord, in charge of my life,
and make me more aware of Your power and Your presence.
God, please do what I cannot do myself.
In Jesus's name we pray,
Amen.

SESSION

4

OVERCOMING LIES
(CONTINUED)

READ: *HUSH*, CHAPTERS FIVE AND SIX

SOUL WORK

Digging Deep

Look up John 8:31-32 and write it below:

Depending on the version of the Bible you used, you most likely recorded the first part of verse 31 as "if you continue in" or "if you remain faithful to," or "if you hold to." Although the choice of words may vary, they all mean the same thing. Jesus is saying that by understanding and obeying His teachings, we can know the truth, which is the only thing that can set us free.

Jesus was having a conversation with the religious leaders of the time. Although they were listening to Him with their ears, what Jesus said didn't penetrate their understanding because they didn't want to believe or obey Him. His words were full of truth and life, but His teaching wasn't falling on fertile soil. Truth couldn't make a difference in their lives because they weren't willing to let it sink in.

Jesus wants you to allow His love and truth to penetrate your heart. If you open your heart to Him, He will enlighten your understanding, and if you cling to His revealed truth, it will set you free. Doesn't that sound amazing?

Jesus goes on to say that the religious leaders rejected the truth because the devil was their father and they wanted to do what he told them to do, not what God wanted them to do (John 8:44). This enemy is Satan, "the father of lies," and he doesn't want you to know the truth or hold on to it so it can set you free. He wants to keep you captive.

Have you ever felt bombarded by accusing, discouraging thoughts? Maybe they're accusing thoughts about your abuse. Maybe they're discouraging thoughts about your life. That is the enemy. He loves to keep your attention on anything that will bring you down, to keep you frozen in your tracks and unable to embrace the truth and freedom that Jesus wants for you.

> "The Lord has given us everything we need to overcome the devil and his lies. Because He Himself had to do battle with Satan, He knows who and what we're dealing with." (*Hush*, 82)

It's really important to recognize that the lies that play over and over in your mind are not from God and that the key to overcoming them is knowing the truth of God's Word.

Making It Personal

Write down one or two of the lies that seem to play over and over in your mind. If you need some help getting started, review the ones on pages 76-79 in *Hush* and see if you relate to any of them. Or think about the last time you had a really bad day. What were the discouraging lies you were hearing inside of you?

Lie:

Lie:

Now imagine that Jesus is standing in front of you, holding your hands in His, as the enemy begins to attack you with these lies. What do you think Jesus would say in your defense? What would the truth sound like from Him?

Truth:

Truth:

Below is a list of verses to help you find truths to replace lies. You can use this list or others that you find meaningful. Write out the verse in the form of a truth that applies to you, and then read it out loud. Be mindful of any lies you've believed about God and be willing to admit that to yourself and to Him.

Psalm 17:8

Psalm 35:22-24

Isaiah 46:4

Matthew 25:34

Romans 8:1

2 Corinthians 12:10

Philippians 1:6

Philippians 3:14

Colossians 1:13-14

1 John 4:18

"One of the greatest gifts God has given you is the power to choose . . . . If you truly want to be healed, choose to truly believe God. His truth is the truth that sets you free." (*Hush*, 85)

In John 8:31-32, Jesus reminds us that our freedom is found knowing and holding onto the truth. We have to *choose* to hold on to the truths we've written out. Choosing truth sets us free.

Sometime this week, go outside and find a smooth flat stone. Plan to bring it with you to your next group meeting.

Wisdom from the Word

In Ephesians 6, the apostle Paul tells us that we are engaged in a spiritual war with satanic forces and then gives us practical advice about how we can protect ourselves from their attacks. He encourages us to be strong in the Lord, and in His power—not our own, as we learned in the last session—and says that to do this, we need to put on the full armor of God. Then he describes what that armor looks like and explains what each piece means.

Read verses 10-18, fill in the blanks, and write a sentence or two about what these concepts mean to you and how they relate to your healing journey.

The belt of

The breastplate of

Feet fitted with

The shield of

The helmet of

The sword of

What does Paul say we are to do once we've put on the armor of God?

Opening Up

Picture yourself sitting in the park, wearing headphones and listening over and over to a recording of the lies Satan has told you about your abuse and yourself. Share with someone you trust what it sounds like and how it makes you feel. Ask your friend to speak truth to that song of lies. As you listen to your friend, envision yourself deleting that old song from your playlist and replacing it with a new tune—one that speaks words of truth, love, affirmation, and encouragement for the journey ahead. Put that new song on repeat and move ahead!

CIRCLE WORK

Getting Real

Consider sharing with the group your answers to these questions:

- ☐ What do you think is the biggest lie you've embraced in the past?
- ☐ What has believing it cost you?
- ☐ Has Satan tried to make you believe a lie about God?

Read aloud the last two paragraphs of page 97 and discuss.

Allow your circle to provide feedback and encouragement and write down some of their comments.

Discuss the armor of God with your group and consider answering this question based on your own life: What piece of the armor do you seem to need the most lately and why?

Story Time

As others in your group are sharing, pray for them. Afterwards, offer your reaction with the group. Remember to be validating, comforting, loving, and encouraging. If you haven't shared during Story Time yet but feel that you are just about ready to, talk to your leader about signing up to tell it at the next session.

Creative Moment

Think about the biggest lie you've ever believed about God. Try to sum up the lie in one word. Write the lie on one side of the stone you brought with you, and then flip the stone over and on the other side write one word that sums up the truth that refutes the lie. Going around the circle, have a quick show-and-tell time, reading aloud the words you have written. Once you are home, put the stone in a visible location. In the coming week, every time you see the stone, ask the Lord to break the power of the lie and replace it with the truth.

Prayer Ministry

Proverbs tells us that our words have the power of life and death. Many of us who have experienced abuse have listened to lies from our abusers as well as from Satan, the ultimate abuser. So during prayer time today, let's bless each other with our words. This is our chance to be voices of life and hope and truth and love and light. Here's how you do it.

If there are more than three people in your group, consider breaking into groups of two or three. In each group, pray for each person one at a time. Ask the person who is receiving prayer if you can put your hand on her shoulder, arm, or another appropriate place. (It's always good to ask for permission to do this because for some of us this can trigger negative reactions due to our abuse.) Then be silent for a moment. Don't rush it. Ask the Lord to speak to you about the person you're going to pray for. Consider the lie that she shared earlier and think about what you would say if you were the one speaking truth to the lie.

For example, if someone has believed the lie that "No one could love me, especially God," you might pray like this: *"I bless you, _____ (name), with the truth that you are loved deeply. The God who made you loves you, and He finds joy in who you are. I bless the lovable things about you: that you are such a great listener, that you have a warm and compassionate heart, that you are easy to love."* Then ask: *"God, would you cause _____(her name) to come out of agreement with the lie that she is unlovable, especially to You, and remind her of the truth in these blessings that we have just prayed over her when she needs to remember it most. Amen."*

SESSION 5

ACCEPTING
FREEDOM THROUGH
FORGIVENESS

READ: *HUSH*, CHAPTERS SEVEN AND EIGHT

SOUL WORK

This week you'll begin to prepare yourself to take the third major step in moving from silence to healing: forgiving those who have hurt you. I say "begin to prepare" because this can be a long process, and to be authentic, it can't be rushed. But as long as it may take and as difficult as it might be, forgiveness is absolutely essential in freeing you from the chains that have kept you bound in a pit of pain. Two of the main obstacles that can keep you from forgiving are misconceptions about forgiveness and deep-seated anger, so let's take some time to focus on these issues.

Digging Deep

What has "forgiveness" meant to you in the past? How would you define it? What does it mean to truly forgive someone?

Did you personally relate to any of the people in the stories in chapters 7 and 8? If so, who and why? If you didn't relate to any of them, write about what makes you feel so different from them.

Did these chapters cause you to question what you have believed about forgiveness? If so, in what way? If not, why do you think this is so?

One of the main things that keeps survivors stuck in misconceptions about forgiveness is deep-seated anger at our abuser. Maybe you are beginning to understand forgiveness better, but this nagging issue keeps coming up: *What do I do with all of this anger? I am so angry!* Part of being angry at someone who has hurt you is the desire for revenge. I think that's a normal human response, but it's self-defeating because it won't bring us the freedom and peace we long for.

> "To continue moving forward on our healing journey, we have to understand why it's so important to forgive . . ."
> (*Hush*, 102)

Survivors often believe that by withholding forgiveness, we're getting back our control or taking justice into our own hands, but in the end it never makes us feel better. In *Hush*, I say that "unforgivingness doesn't hurt the one who harmed you; it only hurts you." How do you feel about this statement? Do you believe it?

Forgiveness isn't about the person who hurt you; it's about you, your heart, your health, and your future. And forgiveness isn't the same as reconciliation. Write in your own words the difference between the two.

Darcy's story of attempting to reconcile with her abuser and his unwillingness to repent shows us that she still had the option of extending forgiveness because it had nothing to do with her abuser's response. When I reached the point in my healing where I felt ready to take a huge step forward and forgive my abuser, he wasn't even alive. That didn't mean I couldn't go forward. It only emphasized the fact that forgiveness isn't about the perpetrator. It's about breaking the power of abuse that keeps us chained to our abuser. Forgiveness frees us to continue moving toward the light up ahead.

So how can we get to the point where we're ready to forgive our abuser and others who have hurt us? How do we come to understand what forgiveness really is and let go of our anger so that we can truly forgive? The first thing we must do is to accept God's forgiveness for our own sins.

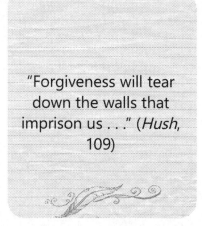

"Forgiveness will tear down the walls that imprison us . . ." (*Hush*, 109)

Hear me out: Although the abuse that happened to us was *not* our fault or our sin, we ourselves are not perfect. God says that all have sinned (Romans 3:23), and that includes every one of us. In His love for us, God sent His Son to pay the penalty for our sins in order to reconcile us to Himself, bringing us into a relationship with Him. As a result of Jesus's death on the Cross, God now offers His forgiveness to anyone who seeks Him and asks for it. When we ask for and accept God's forgiveness, He enlightens our understanding about forgiveness and empowers us to be able to forgive others.

With regard to your relationship with God, what is His job when it comes to forgiveness? What do you need to do?

Wisdom from the Word

Read Matthew 6: 9-18.

This section of Scripture includes what is often called the Lord's Prayer, a model prayer in which Jesus teaches us how to pray. Verses 12, 14, and 15 show that asking God for forgiveness and extending forgiveness to others are two sides of the same coin.

As I read these verses from the perspective of a survivor, I can picture myself still connected to my abuser by a cord. I see Jesus in the distance and long to be near Him, but the cord keeps me running in place and getting no closer to Him or the freedom He can give me. Only forgiveness can cut the cord and free me to run forward.

In Romans 12:19, God reminds us that it's not our job to get even. He is the Judge; it's His prerogative to execute justice and take revenge.

I know that's hard to hear and really hard to accept sometimes, but when you harbor anger and the desire for revenge, you allow the enemy to come in and take up residence inside of you.

I believe there is such a thing as healthy anger—like being angry at the sin committed against you! However, we are not to sin as a result of our anger. In Ephesians 4:22, the apostle Paul challenges us to "put on a new self"—one that walks in freedom and health, not in bitterness and anger.

> "Complain if you must, but don't lash out. Keep your mouth shut, and let your heart do the talking. Build your case before God and wait for his verdict."
> (Psalm 4:4, msg)

God has a plan and a purpose for your life, and He is calling you to walk in it. (Romans 8:28). You didn't get to choose what happened to you in your past, but you do get to choose to take this next step. By choosing to accept God's forgiveness and extend forgiveness to others, you are choosing to move forward on your healing journey and accepting the freedom I know you're longing for.

Remember:

- ☐ In Jesus, I am forgiven! (Ephesians 1:7)
- ☐ In Jesus, I am rescued, redeemed, and forgiven! (Colossians 1:13-15)
- ☐ In Jesus, I have been cleansed of my past! (2 Peter 1:9)
- ☐ Because of Jesus, I choose love and live in the light! (1 John 2:10)

Plan to bring your favorite blanket to your next group meeting.

CIRCLE WORK

Getting Real

Discuss your answers to the following questions with the members of your circle.

- [ ] What is your reaction to the stories you read in *Hush* this week?
- [ ] Do you think you now have a better understanding of what forgiveness is?

Story Time

Do you have a positive experience of forgiveness you can share with the group? It could be the moment when you first forgave someone, it could be a process of forgiveness you have gone through, or it could be an experience of being forgiven. Share if you are willing.

If there are more survivors willing to break the silence and share their stories of abuse, this is also the time for that. Remember: this is a safe place to break the silence and regain your voice.

Creative Moment

Write a letter to your abuser. No one has to read this, and you will probably not give this letter to him or her. This is ultimately not about your abuser or anyone else. It's about you and God. Get real about the pain your abuser's sin has caused. Tell him that you aren't minimizing what he did, but that you are choosing to forgive him. Tell her that you are severing the tie that unforgivingness has had on you and that you are releasing her to Jesus to be dealt with. Use as colorful language as you feel is needed to release some anger or to name the sin and its effects. Don't filter your words or emotion; just be perfectly honest.

If you feel ready to cut the cord binding you to your abuser's control and the pain he or she has caused, consider writing a statement of forgiveness in your own words. State why you are making this decision and what you hope to gain from it. If you don't finish during your group's time together, plan to finish as you do your 'Soul Work' in the week ahead.

Prayer Ministry

Zephaniah 3:17 talks about how God rejoices over us and delights in us. The Hebrew word for "rejoice over" paints a picture of Him "twirling in circles" over us. Can you imagine God loving you so much that he gets that excited about you? It's so awesome!

The verse also says that God quiets us with his love. Turn down the lights in the room. Play soft music. Grab the blanket you brought with you, wrap it around yourself, and imagine that God is wrapping you in His love. Sit quietly in His presence and ask Him to reveal His love to you. Ask him to quiet any anger you might feel toward your abuser with the power of His peaceful, loving embrace. If you feel as though God has spoken something to your heart, consider sharing that experience with your circle.

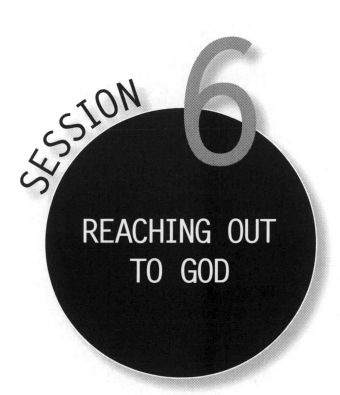

SESSION 6

REACHING OUT
TO GOD

READ: *HUSH*, CHAPTERS NINE AND TEN

SOUL WORK

Today we are going to practice the presence of God.

As we get started, I want you to pause for a moment, quiet your mind, and take a cleansing breath. Concentrate on breathing deeply-in and then out. Now think about that breath. Think about your lungs. Think about what they do over and over every minute of every day to keep you breathing. Think about how they do this without you ever thinking about it. Unless there's a problem, you just take this process for granted, right?

Consider how your Heavenly Father created this amazing system to keep you alive. The same amazing God who filled the ocean and painted the sky gave you this breath (Isaiah 42:5). And He has put a similar spiritual system in place for you. Although you aren't always aware of it, He is as close to you as the air you breathe.

This week I want you to make a point of taking time out of your busy schedule to be still and invite God into your everyday life. This is one way we can begin to practice the presence of God. When we make it a priority to connect with God, no matter where we are or what is going on around us, our minds can find rest, and our hearts can find freedom and fullness of life.

Digging Deep

In chapter 9 of *Hush*, I make the point that many survivors of abuse find it hard to accept the truth that no other human being can give them all they need to feel complete. No matter how close our relationship with another person, we have to admit that deep inside we long for something more. That's how God made us. We have a hole in our heart, a void that only He can fill.

What is your reaction to what I wrote in the book? Be honest. No one is going to judge you. This is just about getting real with yourself and God.

Have you allowed God to fill that empty place in your heart? Do you feel that He is as close as the air you breathe? If not, perhaps you have been trying to fill the void with other people or with things.

Write down the names of some of the people in your life you've allowed to take up residence in the place that only God's love can fill.

"The belief that any human being can meet all our needs is a delusion."
(*Hush*, 138)

What has been the outcome?

Perhaps it hasn't been a person who has taken God's place in your heart. Perhaps it has been things or ways of coping. Survivors of abuse carry a lot of baggage, which we often fill with things that, while we think they will meet our needs, only end up hurting us more. Page 129 describes some of this kind of baggage. Have you tucked any of these things into your personal carry-on? List any that you feel apply to you.

Picture yourself taking out some of the negative thoughts or habits you carry around in your baggage and replacing them with things that would make you feel fulfilled and alive. What would that replacement be? What would make you feel worthy? Valued? What are the dreams you hold inside? Write down some things you would prefer to fill your suitcase with. Answer any of these questions when you feel ready to and be as real as you can.

Wisdom from the Word

The Bible says, "We know and rely on the love God has for us. God is love. Whoever lives in love lives in God, and God in them" (1 John 4:16). What this verse tells us is that if we allow God to fill the hole in our heart, three things will happen:

1. We will know God's love.
2. We will rely on God's love.
3. We will live in God's love.

It's only when we know, rely upon, and live in God's love that we're able to truly love others and not expect them—whether friends, mentors, spouses, parents, siblings, children, or lovers—to fill the place in us that is meant for God.

It can be really easy to put someone or something in the place that God longs to fill. That's why we must let the truth of His love sink in deep, just as we must fill our lungs with pure, fresh air to stay alive and well. Otherwise, we'll always be looking to someone or something else for love and acceptance, always ending up confused, disillusioned, and heartsick.

So, how do we get to know, rely upon, and live in God's love? How do we let it sink into our heart and let Him fill us? The answer is really quite simple: We begin by believing what God's Word says—that He is always near and that we can approach Him confidently, knowing that He wants to hear from us and help us.

> "Even if it hurts and takes time, the truth will ultimately set you free." (*Hush*, 150)

This isn't the game of hide-and-seek we played in childhood or the drama of the dating scene. It's a relationship we can engage in with confidence. No matter who we think we are or who we believe we have become, no matter what we have done, no matter what has been done to us, the Lord promises us that He is always near. He sees us and He loves us. He is always extending His hand to us. And it isn't a hand of rebuke or discipline, as abuse survivors might expect, but a hand of compassion and care, of warmth and welcome.

Close your eyes, take a couple cleansing breaths, and silently invite the Lord to join you as you open your Bible and read the following verses. Fill in the blanks of these paraphrases with the word you think best fits the meaning:

- Deuteronomy 4:7: He is _____ me whenever I pray.
- Psalm 34:18: He is _____ to the brokenhearted and _____ those who are crushed in spirit.
- Jeremiah 23:23: He is _____ me wherever I am.
- Ephesians 3:12: Through faith on Jesus, I can approach God with _____.
- Hebrews 4:16: God wants me to come to Him _____ to find help in times of need.
- 1 John 5:14: As a child of God, I have _____ in approaching Him.

Part of what it means to be in close human relationships is that we're free to open up to other people no matter what is on our heart, knowing they are always near, wanting to help us all they can and give us what we need.

Psalm 37:4 says, "Delight yourself in the Lord, and he will give you the desires of your heart." The word used for "delight" here comes from the Hebrew word for "petition" or "request." It's connected to what we've been talking about: knowing, relying on, and living in God's love, as it refers to seeking and desiring God first and above everyone and everything else. God's Word promises us that He really wants to hear about our deepest feelings and listen to the petitions of our heart and soul.

And it isn't as if God is listening while He is busy doing other things—like I tend to do! He's listening with complete attention. He hears every word with a heart of mercy, grace, and kindness and with the intention of granting our request, according to His will.

Because of His great love for you, God wants to meet your needs and grant your requests. He promises to grant any petition that will result in the very best for you. Does knowing that make you feel more confident to approach God and share with Him the desires of your heart? Does it make you want to invite Him into your sacred spaces and reveal your innermost thoughts and feelings? If so, tell Him!

What is the desire of your heart? What is your request?

God's Word tells us that we can be bold and free in His presence. We are safe with Him! We can breathe deeply around Him, we can be vulnerable, and we can be completely real with Him. As we do, His presence, truth, grace, love, and mercy will come in; He will replace all the hurtful things in our suitcase with good stuff. And He promises that as our journey continues, He will walk with us, picking up the pieces of our brokenness and putting us back together as we take each step forward.

Opening Up

In Matthew 22, Jesus was asked by the religious leaders of the day which of God's commandments was the most important. Jesus didn't stop to think about His answer; He didn't skip a beat. He told them that the most important commandment is to love God with all their heart (emotions), soul (spiritual self), and mind (thoughts). He knew that when we put someone or something before Him, we will inevitably be disappointed. To prevent that, we need to focus on relating to God—on His nearness, His love, and the work He is doing in us.

Jesus didn't stop there. He went on to say that we are to love other people as much as we love ourselves. Once we are in a close, personal relationship with God, we can focus on all He wants to do for others through us. As we will learn more about in the week ahead, we get to be a part of His message of love to the world!

Creative Moment

This week you'll prepare for the group session by completing the "Creative Moment" before you meet with your circle. One day this week climb into your bathtub and fill it with water as high as you can. While the tub is filling, imagine that the water is God's love. Or you may feel more comfortable standing in the shower and picturing God's love pouring down over you. As you lie there soaking in it, or stand there being surrounded in it, ask the Lord to fill you with a sense of His love for you—not just His love generally, but His love for *you*, specifically.

Next, close your eyes and begin to offer your body to Him. Offer Him the parts that you are ashamed of because of the wrong done to you through abuse. Ask Him to heal you and cleanse you from the effects of the abuse. Ask Him to restore every part of you. Next, begin to offer other parts of yourself to Him—your mind, your hands, your eyes, your words, whatever you feel led to offer—and invite Him to heal and restore each part of your being.

If you're comfortable doing so, dunk your head under water. Imagine that the Lord's love is washing over you and enveloping you. Then sit up and let water drain out of the tub, or if you chose to shower, slowly turn it off. Ask the Lord to cast every sin (your sin and the sin against you) far from you. As you watch it all go down the drain, thank Him for the amazing gift of healing, cleansing, and forgiveness.

CIRCLE WORK

Getting Real

Discuss your answers to any of the following questions that resonate with you.

- ☐ What are your reactions to the stories you read in *Hush* this week? Did you relate to any particular one?
- ☐ Have you experienced a broken or roller-coaster relationship like the ones described in chapters 9 and 10? Share some of what that relationship felt like.
- ☐ What on your personal list of old baggage do you want to get rid of?
- ☐ What is something positive you want to put in your suitcase for the road ahead?
- ☐ What is one of your dreams for the future?
- ☐ How did the "Creative Moment" make you feel?

Story Time

If any members of your circle are ready to share their story, now is a great time to give them your attention and let them know they are safe to do so. Validate them, love them, and encourage them. Talking about our experiences takes a ton of courage, and we all need to be reminded of that.

Prayer Ministry

Take a moment to consider the last several weeks of prayer ministry time. Reflect on anything that made you feel anxious. Think of how hard it was to trust the others in your group. Have you seen changes in yourself? Has God taught you to pray? Have you begun to feel that He is always near? How do you think the Lord has used you in the lives of your circle members over the past few weeks?

Take a few minutes together to thank the Lord out loud for the ways He has been restoring you and your voice. Thank Him for the changes you notice in yourself and the individuals around you. Don't worry about saying anything eloquent or "spiritual." Just talk with God normally, as you would with a friend.

Start with, *"Jesus, thank You so much for . . .*

SESSION 7

REACHING OUT
TO OTHERS

READ: *HUSH*, CHAPTER ELEVEN

SOUL WORK

This week, our final week of the *SOAR* study, takes us to the fourth major step in moving from silence to healing: making a difference.

In walking through this study, you have made an incredibly important commitment. I'm not only proud of you, but also confident that the Lord has met you in some way in this sacred time of soul work and circle work. And, just as I believe His healing comfort has entered your life, I have no doubt that someone else will experience that same comfort through you as you continue on this journey.

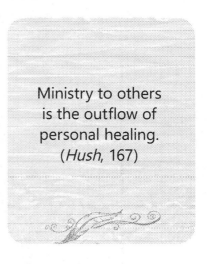

Ministry to others is the outflow of personal healing. (*Hush*, 167)

Digging Deep

Comfort. What picture or thoughts come to mind when you hear or read that word? Draw it or explain it in words.

Describe a time in your life when you felt comforted.

On page 164 in *Hush*, I say that Satan uses lies to keep us from reaching out to help or comfort others. Are there any lies that may have been keeping you from reaching out? Explain.

Think about how you would answer these questions:

- ☐ How has God gifted you? What talents do you have?
- ☐ What are your passions? What do you enjoy doing in your free time?
- ☐ With what kind of people do you interact with on a regular basis?
- ☐ How might God want you to use your talents and personality to make an impact on these people?

Reaching out can be as simple as finding ways to raise money for a local shelter, putting posters around your community to raise awareness, initiating an event with speakers and resources, or getting your local church/college/school/prison to start a support group for survivors of abuse based on the SOAR curriculum. It can also mean helping a single mom with childcare or volunteering for a local child advocacy center. Above all else, it means being intentional in teaching your kids about health and safety and making sure you, yourself, are actively healing and being the best person, parent, worker, and friend that you can be.

Pray about all of this. Ask the Lord to make you sensitive to His work. Invite Him to give you a creative vision of how you can walk out this fourth step on your journey of moving from silence to healing. Write down whatever comes to your mind and heart.

Wisdom from the Word

Read 2 Corinthians 1:3-4.

The words *comfort* and *comforts* mean two different things here.

Comfort refers to acts of encouraging and strengthening. Paul, who wrote this letter, really wanted the Corinthian believers—and Christians today—to be encouraged and strengthened through their relationship with Jesus. So he's writing about the comfort we receive, why we receive it, and from whom it comes. He says that it is God who meets our need for comfort and that He is, in fact, the God of all comfort.

What does that mean to you? What would you like it to mean for you? Consider writing directly to God here.

The word *comforts* relates more to the physical act of comforting. It's about being at someone's side. When God meets us in our neediness, when He sits next to us in our sorrow, He offers us things like strength, encouragement, endurance, peace, and faithful friendship. He gives us these comforts freely, but He also expects us to pass them on to others. As He meets us in our brokenness, He perfects our testimony, and when we share it, it makes His redemption known, bringing beauty out of ashes (Isaiah 61:3).

Skipping ahead a few chapters in 2 Corinthians, we come to 7:6, which shows us that we can be encouraged even as we comfort others. When we share our story, others will share their stories. And just as our healing began by breaking the silence, so can theirs.

Even more amazing is that you can find rest in knowing that while He is using you as His vessel in all of this incredible work, He alone is our ultimate savior and healer. This means that you can lead others to break the silence and comfort them with the comfort you have received—all without feeling that you need to fix them. This gives you the freedom to do the good work He has prepared for you, while He handles the hardest part.

> His healing waters have showered you, and now you have a well for others to draw from. (*Hush*, 167)

There are many stories in the Bible about people who had evil things happen to them, yet God still used them to bring about great things that advanced His kingdom. One of my favorites is Joseph. (If you want to spend some extra time reading his amazing story, grab your Bible and an espresso and read Genesis chapters 37 and 39-45).

Poor Joseph went through a lot while he was growing up, and I'm certain he needed a serious amount of healing and comfort to deal with the pain of it. You and I have been through a lot, too, and I'm certain God has a vision for our lives just as He had for Joseph's. You may not know what God's plan for your life looks like yet. You may once have had a vision of what life could be like for you, but because of your abuse you really don't think it's possible and that it's just a silly dream. But what if that vision really is from God? Suppose that, like Joseph's dream, it's God's plan for your life. No matter the circumstances of your life, if God has planted a dream within you, He is able to carry it out. The Lord has huge plans for you, friend!

Fill in the blanks:

Mark 10:27: Jesus looked at them and said, "With man this is _____, but not with God; _____ _____with God."

Philippians 4:13: I can do _____through him who gives me _____

Romans 8:28: And we _____that in all things God works for the _____of those who _____Him, who have been called according to His _____

2 Corinthians 12:9: But he said to me, "My grace is _____ for you, for my power is made _____ in weakness."

Ephesians 2:10: For we are God's handiwork, created in Christ Jesus to do _____, which God prepared in _____ for us to do.

Christ is sufficient. Through Him, we are renewed and recreated for a purpose. Isn't it exciting to know that God created good works for us to do? I hope you are beginning to feel grounded in your calling as a child of God and are beginning to ask, "What are those good works God has created for me to do?" I like to compare searching for these things to going on an Easter egg hunt—but that's just me!

Read Isaiah 6:8 and Matthew 25:35-40 and really let those verses sink into your heart. Jesus calls each one of us to carry His kingdom message of love forward—and we must respond! God is calling us to step out of our hiding place, look around, and be His hands and feet to the world around us. There's plenty of work to do, plenty of people in need of true love and genuine comfort, plenty of injustice to overcome. We can't just stew in our problems or settle for our own healing; we must step out, look for ways to be an answer in this dark world, and take action!

> No matter where you are, or what your profession is, you are surrounded by hurting people. (*Hush*, 166)

Write about an experience you've had in the past when you offered comfort to someone. What was that person dealing with? How did you approach him or her? What did you do or say?

Did you feel you were giving this person the same comfort you had once received? Could you relate to this person in any way?

How did this person receive your comfort? And how did you feel about it then? How do you feel about it now?

Looking Back

Healing from the effects of childhood sexual abuse is no easy task. It takes courage—and you should be proud of yourself for how far you've come!

Looking back over the course of these past seven sessions, ask yourself if your experience of God is different than when you first began. Has God comforted you? Did He use a specific person in your circle to speak to your heart or mind to bring healing, truth, courage, or comfort?

Spend some time reflecting on this and then set aside a good chunk of quiet time to journal your thoughts.

Looking Ahead

For our circle work this week, bring a photo of yourself taken at the age you were when you experienced abuse.

In the course of this study, has God placed a person on your heart you might consider reaching out to with the same comfort you have received? If so, write down that name (or names).

Brainstorm some ways you could begin to reach out to these people and then list your ideas here:

God wants to use you in mighty ways. Your mess can become His message. Your health and your purpose could blossom from the healing of your pain. God is restoring your voice. Free your heart to receive His comfort. Renew your mind to be filled with His wisdom and truth. Open your eyes and ears to find the hurting ones around you. Finally, surrender your hands, purse, and schedule to meet those who could use a little comfort, support, and encouragement today.

CIRCLE WORK

Getting Real

Go through the Soul Work portion of this week's study and share some of the things you've journaled.

Story Time

Share with the circle how you feel God might be calling you to make a difference in the world or in the life of a specific person. Share stories of how God has already used you and your testimony. Encourage one another.

Creative Moment

Share with the circle the picture of yourself at the age you were when you were abused. Each member of the circle will say something they notice about that little girl. Respond to each observation with "thank you." Once everyone has done this, go around the circle again. This time everyone will respond with an encouragement or blessing about what they see in the survivor today or a positive change they have noticed in the past seven weeks. Again, say only "thank you," while making every effort to receive the words as true.

Allow a good amount of time for this exercise and don't rush it.

Prayer Ministry

Everyone close your eyes and pray silently while the leader reads the following prompts:

- ☐ Try to remember how liberating it was when someone else broke the silence.
- ☐ Now picture yourself being the one to give someone else that feeling of freedom.
- ☐ Ask God to show you a person you might begin to reach out to outside this circle. If you already know who that is, ask for an opportunity to start that dialogue.
- ☐ Ask Him to bring to your mind the name of one person you could invite to read *Hush*.
- ☐ Ask Him to show you one person who is in need of comfort right now. He or she could be a victim of abuse or just be going through a dark time.
- ☐ What is one thing that you could commit to do this month?

Close in prayer by having the leader pray a blessing over the group as wounded healers.

Consider planning a fun outing in the next month for everyone to gather and enjoy community together and catch up on life.

"Do you not know?

Have you not heard?

The Lord is the everlasting God,

the Creator of the ends of the earth.

He will not grow tired or weary,

and his understanding no one can fathom.

He gives strength to the weary

and increases the power of the weak.

Even youths grow tired and weary,

and young men stumble and fall;

but those who hope in the Lord

will renew their strength.

They will soar on wings like eagles;

they will run and not grow weary,

they will walk and not be faint"

(Isaiah 40:28-31)

It has been an honor to walk with you these past seven weeks. May God continue to bless your journey ahead as you go forth with Jesus and SOAR!

A WORD TO LEADERS

As a leader, your role is to create a safe environment, one that will empower and encourage survivors to share. Confidentiality is of utmost importance in a *SOAR* group, as it's what creates a safe space for sharing. *SOAR* leaders should teach and enforce this at the initial introductory meeting and bring it up throughout the following seven sessions. It's critical to keep the confidences of group members and to impress on them the necessity of maintaining the confidential nature of privileged information in the group. The only time a leader may step outside of the confines of confidentiality is when a group member is at immediate risk of serious harm to themself or others.

In your initial meeting, you'll want to establish some important boundaries. *SOAR* members need to know that they can cry. They can laugh. They can be angry. They can be honest. They can choose to share hard things. Or they can choose to not share at all. But two things they cannot do. One is to discuss issues that do not pertain to the study or relate to abuse; the other is to repeat anything that happens in the group to someone outside of the group. What is shared in the group stays in the group. No member is to share with someone outside of the group any information that would identify anyone as a group member of *SOAR*.

Each group member's role is vital in contributing to a feeling of safety within the circle. Each has the right to have her voice heard. You may not always agree with what is being said or shared, or you may not be able to relate to everyone's story. However, it's important to show that you value your circle members and their willingness to share by protecting their identity and what they share.

Group members themselves should establish any other guidelines and ground rules. As a leader, you should make up possible scenarios and have group members decide what is or is not acceptable. This will help build trust within the group and help them bond, which is essential for a group to be successful.

Because the topics addressed in the group can elicit strong emotions and reactions, you should either advise group members to be involved in personal therapy or require that they have done some work in personal therapy prior to participating in the group. If and when group members experience overwhelming emotions, they should contact both the group leader and their personal therapist. If they are not currently in therapy, in the introductory meeting you can provide contact information for counselors in the local area. These are safe others who can assist them when the journey gets too difficult for them to travel alone.

Now for a few recommendations about group dynamics.

It would be best to keep group size to either eight members with one leader, or ten members and two coleaders. No new members can be added to the *SOAR* group after the first session. Adding new members breaks down trust, confidentiality, and the opportunity for deep, meaningful community that this group can provide. If new people want to join, ask them to add their name to a waiting a list for a new group.

Attendance is vital. Ask all participants to take the group seriously by committing to all seven sessions and arriving on time. This leads to feelings of safety and trust within the group. Expect the Circle Work to take from one and a half to two hours each week. There will be weeks when you run out of time, but do your best to end on time no matter how far you get through the material. This shows respect for others' boundaries and schedules and keeps the group healthy.

The group can set up the room however they like. We recommend a circle or oval of chairs with a couple of tables and chairs set up outside of the circle for the "creative moment" activity, in which we often use art as a form of therapy. You may want to have soft music playing in the background. You might even have a few questions written on a board so that when the members arrive, they can journal as they are waiting for group to begin. This can sometimes help alleviate feelings of awkwardness or anxiety.

It is important for every group session to begin with our short video openers. The seven *SOAR* videos are hosted by me and include some of my survivor friends sharing their stories. They will help break the ice by encouraging sharing and bring a level of comfort and understanding as you begin each group session. You can purchase the *SOAR* DVD or download the short films through our online store at iamonevoice.org. Sample *SOAR* group registration forms and confidentiality agreements can also be downloaded from the online store.

Lastly, thank you for your compassion and care for survivors of sexual abuse and for your commitment to creating a safe space where they can journey toward healing together. I am praying for you!

ACKNOWLEDGMENTS

An enormous thank you to all of the sexual abuse survivors, counselors, pastors, and leaders who have supported the message in my first book, *Hush,* and have begged me to make this workbook and group guide possible. I wouldn't have done this without your courage to find deeper healing and your passion to get more out of life. Your support has truly kept me moving.

Special love and gratitude to the amazing people who have been so valuable in the preparation of this project. Enormous gratitude to Erin George for believing in me and in this book and for assisting me so selflessly in research, brainstorming, planning, prayer-anything that would make this workbook and the first *SOAR* group a meaningful experience for all. A great big thank you to my dear friend Sara Carlisle for her fresh insights and ideas, specifically with creative moments and in helping construct prayers for Circle Work.

Thank you, Christen Cushing, for your sweet friendship and for sharing your creative talents to design the cover for this workbook. Thanks to my amazing editor, Judith St. Pierre, for all she does to help clarify my voice when it's too rough and scattered and for her commitment to me, even in her retirement.

Thanks to an incredible film crew from Posthouse for producing the videos for all seven *SOAR* group sessions. Rick Green, Tim Flaherty, John Masserella and Scott Baldner got behind this project with belief, compassion, and generosity. I'm so grateful for their talent and work, as well as all the fun we had along the way. Thanks, guys!

I would like to thank all of my precious survivor friends who courageously shared their stories in the group session videos and those who journeyed with me through the very first *SOAR* group at Vineyard Columbus, my church home. Thank you, Solena Helm, for helping me lead the group, for drafting administrative forms and for sharing so transparently in the group and the film. Deep admiration and appreciation for Mary O'Brien as she courageously walked through the first SOAR group as a participant, then stepped into leading SOAR groups, and now is a powerful voice alongside mine on the OneVOICE podcast. God has given me such a gift.

I want to also give a shout-out to Life Outreach International for providing film footage from my work in Cambodia. I'm so honored to have their supportive partnership in bringing hope to those that are hurting around the world. You have become like family—thanks for linking arms with me in this mission!

Thank you, Moody Publishers, who believed in me and my message since the beginning and turned *Hush* into a real book that would eventually change so many lives.

Thank you to Morven Baker, Michelle Garrett and Dana Kasper for sharing wise feedback on the manuscript from a counselor's perspective and to Sharon Walls, my counselor, for giving such valuable support and encouragement to me on my personal healing journey. And thanks to those trusted loved ones who helped care for my kiddos so I could write.

The deepest of thanks to Matt and our boys, my mom and stepdad, my dad and stepmom, my close friends, family and my personal circle of inspiration for supporting me, cheering for me, being patient with me, speaking truth in love to me, and praying for me as I continue to heal and grow and walk out the calling God has given me. You are a collection of feathers in my wings, enabling me to SOAR as a voice in fighting injustice and giving hope to survivors around the world.

A portion of the proceeds from this book will be donated to the OneVOICE mission to stop child sex trafficking.

iamonevoice.org

onevoice4freedom.org

Printed in the United States
By Bookmasters